HOW TO BE A SUCCESSFUL FEMALE ENTREPRENEUR

A Woman Entrepreneur's Guide to Starting and Running a Successful Business

ISAAC GIWA

HOW TO BE A SUCCESSFUL FEMALE ENTERPRENEUR

Copyright © 2017, ISAAC GIWA

Published by

ISGIBSON SERVICES

6, kamoru Adeyemi Street, Ire-Akari Estate, Isolo, Lagos-Nigeria.

P.O. Box 621, Ikeja

Lagos, Nigeria

Tel: 234-1-8023147715

234-1-8036665662

E-mail: isgibsonservices@gmail.com

isaacgiwabooks@gmail.com

NB: All scripture quotations are from the King James Version of the Bible, except otherwise stated.

Contents

1

WOMEN, PURPOSE AND ENTREPRENUERSHIP

There is no entrepreneurial success outside purpose. If you don't know why you are living, you cannot achieve much as an entrepreneur.

Purpose is the original reason for existence. Purpose is the destination. Woman, for you to achieve anything great in life and business, you must discover and identify with your purpose. Most successful women we see in our world today are the ones that have discovered their mission in life. They have discovered the reason for their existence and they stayed with it. Your purpose in life was designed even before you were made and until you discover the purpose, you never experience true success in business. Purpose is the starting point of all great success and achievement. Every product in life is made for a specific purpose. And every object is created to perform a specific function.

Woman, you belong somewhere. You are not an accident and it's your responsibility to find where you belong. You have been separated from your mother's womb to do something and that is the purpose for your living.

Every human being possesses and quietly incubates a secret dream or purpose deposited in their spirit by the creator, a purpose to fulfill on this planet in their life time. This deposit is described in many names like destiny, assignment, mission, and so on. Everyone is created for a particular purpose. Successes begin at the point of locating and walking on your mission in life.

Behind every achievement in business is the force of purpose. Locate where you belong in life and stay there. Your mission in life is the fuel that drives your business to dominate the market.

Purpose is the first, the second and the third law of outstanding accomplishment. Purpose is one of fundamental pillars of business success. You are created for a particular course. And it is that course that will distinguish you in life.

Every great business woman that ever achieved great result in life and business were women of purpose. Success only comes to a person who is committed to a purpose or has a passion to achieve.

As a female entrepreneur, discovering and

pursuing your purpose is your master key for greatness.

DISCOVER YOUR PURPOSE

Firmness of purpose is one of the most necessary sinews of character and one of the best instruments of success. Without it, genius wastes its efforts in a maze of inconsistencies.

Lord chesterfield

Every great woman that has ever ascended to the level of super and unlimited success got there by discovering their particular purpose.

If you mention Mary Kay, what readily comes to mind is beauty product. When you mention the name Oprah winfrey, what comes to mind is television talk show. Halle berry is synonymous with acting. Onyeka onwenu is synonymous with music, while Hilary Clinton is politics.

Martin Luther king Jr. said, "If a man hasn't discovered something that he will die for, he isn't fit to life.

Discovery of purpose is the first, second and the third low for digging your own diamond. A discovery of your life purpose is the gateway to dignity in life. As a business woman, you must settle this in your mind. You cannot live the kind of life you desire until you discover your mission for living. Life will never give you what you want but what you are.

DEGREE IS NOT EQUAL TO SUCCESS

When a woman has not discovered the reason for her existence she will always live in financial crisis. Every woman that has succeeded and made an enviable accomplishment in life and business did so on the platform on the discovery of her purpose.

Don't let your discipline destroy your destiny in life. Don't be a captive of your degrees.

You have a mandate to fulfill and your discovery of that purpose and vigorously pursuing it, is what we call success.

Your purpose in life may be in music, acting, catering service, fashion and beauty, telecommunication, journalist and so on. But the fact is you belong somewhere. You are not an accident and it is your responsibility to find where you belong and until you discover it, you will never experience true success in business.

2

PUT YOUR NATURAL TALENT TO WORK

If you recognize your talents, use them appropriately. Choose a field that uses those talents and you will rise to the top of your field. –Ben Carson.

Entrepreneurial success is real and achievable. You are a potential millionaire. You are too loaded to remain a mediocre. You are smarter and more intelligent than you have ever imagined. You have great talent and potential as a woman entrepreneur to guarantee your success in life and business. You have more wisdom, ability, brain power and creative ability to create a life time of financial abundance. Your ability to use your talent, Think deeply and develop profitable ideas to help you create streams of income and success is unlimited – This means that your ability to succeed greatly as a female entrepreneur is unlimited as well.

Your gifting is a pointer to your purpose in life. Every gift in you is put there by God for your business success. Gifts are deposits. They are the productive activities that naturally flow out of you.

There is no ungifted woman in life. Every woman has some ability in her. All women are gifted and a woman's gift and talent is a point of contact with her purpose in life. You don't have an excuse not to succeed in business.

WHAT ARE YOU GOOD AT?

You have special talent and abilities that make you different from every other person who has ever lived. Take stock of your unique talents and abilities on a regular basis. What is it that you do especially well? What are you good at? What do you do easily and well which is difficult for other people. To make a headway in life and business you must ask yourself "what am I really good at? what will distinguish me and set me apart as special and unique in a lineup of my friends?

Look at the various things you do, what is it that you do that gets you the most compliments and praise from other people?

Successful business women are invariably those who have taken time to identify what they do well and enjoy most. They know what they do that really makes a difference in their lives and they then concentrate on that task or area of activity exclusively.

Consumers in life aren't effective at discovering what is inside of them and then putting this to work. Consumers often spend all that comes to them. They are a dead –end for resources put into their hands. A consumer is like a one –way entrance point for resources. A consumer doesn't provide and is a tramp to the future.

On the other hand successful women in life discover and maximize what has been given to them to create and build more. Successful women think differently about what is within them as well as what they receive in terms of resources. Successful women clearly understand that when their gifts and abilities are discovered, developed and utilized through their life's work. They grow in wealth and success.

CREATING YOUR OWN PRODUCT AND SERVICES

Opportunities for wealth creation are put inside of you through your gifts and talents. Wealth is not simply money put in your pockets. Rather wealth is the ability to be innovative and creative to produce something and then exchange it for money.

All that is needed is to discover what God has placed inside of you. That is where you will find the potential for wealth. Wealth is not in the hand of certain few. Wealth is within each of us through our abilities to produce in life, to use what we have and then multiply it. It is not that God makes rich people or poor people. Rather, God makes people, some decided to be rich while some stayed poor by their own negative choices or indecision.

Poverty is not a gift from God but product of your action. What you do with what you have is what determines the degree of your riches.

VALUE YOURSELF

Many women undervalued their own strength and worth. it is very dangerous to devalue your worth before someone who is in negotiation with you, because of your present circumstances. It is a big mistake when your opponent places move value on your talent and worth than you do yourself. Many individual and cooperate organizations have entered into business negotiations with a very low value for what they had to offer and end up releasing their destiny for almost nothing.

A great man once said, 'it is your sense of value that determines the flow of virtue. What you don't value cannot deliver.

It is very easy to devalue what you have because of familiarity and commonness. When you live with something for so long and always have access to it, you tend to take it for granted. There by losing its value. It is very easy to take for granted what you have around you all the time.

Never take the gifts, talents and ability others value in you for granted. Because it is your principal tool for financial and entrepreneurial success. Next time, you sit before negotiating tables make sure that your opponent does not see more talent and treasure in you than you think you have. When he gets to think that you don't know what you are worth, he would offer you a flattering service package, which he knows is far lower that your worth. A Lot of women get flattered by so little because they don't know the true value or worth of what God has deposited inside them.

3

DISCOVER AND MAXIMIZE YOUR UNIQUENESS.

We are all unique in some special way, but most of us have been taught, pushed and punished into conformity – Brian Sher.

To succeed as an entrepreneur, you must discover and work on your uniqueness. You are unique, peculiar and special. You are designed to bring a unique result in life and business. There is something in you which God has put there to make you outstanding in business. You were designed to be somebody. You are a book to be read and you must show up.

The hall mark of business success is its trade mark. That is what it sells in the market above other unbranded products. And your uniqueness is your trademark as an entrepreneur. your product and services must be branded after your style and uniqueness to give it a touch of peculiarity. Your real place of relevance in business is not in your similarity to another but your uniqueness.

You are a peculiar business woman predestined to be a success; strong, powerful and wonderful. Awaken the star in you. Find out what you have inside of you. Discover what you have been created to achieve in business .Recognize your uniqueness and go for it.

As a woman entrepreneur, your company must discover her strength and uniqueness. You must work towards developing that area and aspire to be the best in that area. You may not be first in that line of business but you can be the best. In maximizing your uniqueness, try to see what you can do to give your business a better shine and a neater presentation.

Do something extra to distinguish yourself in crowd. Carve out a nice for your business and design your business mold yourself. Don't just adopt any style you see around. Let your business carry your own uniqueness or peculiarity. I mean let it be easily identified and associated with you even from afar off.

BE AN ADVENTUROUS WOMAN

Most women that succeeded in business are always adventurous. That is, they always look for new paths where no lion has trodden and which no eagle's eye has seen (job 28:7). As an entrepreneur, you need to be innovative and creative.

A woman called Debbi field in America decided to be baking chocolate- chip cookies to sell. No one – not her family, not her friends, not even her husband, thought this was a good business. Her cookies were soft and chewy. Not crispy like store brands. But she was an adventurous woman. She refuses to give up on her idea. Today, she owned more than five hundreds Mrs. Fields' cookies store in over twenty five states and her company grosses over $300 million annually from over 1000 outlets in nine countries.

Hellen Keller had an adventurous spirit. If she had turned back or giving up, no one would have blamed her but no one would have remembered her name either. Today her name is synonymous with achievements.

As an entrepreneur, you must be excited about new things. you must be fed up with status quo. Stand out and succeed. It's your sense of uniqueness that makes people to do business with you rather than another company. Don't do what everybody is doing. Don't join the crowd, refuse to be a mediocre; choose to be unique and adventurous and you will excel in business.

4

A FEMALE ENTERPRENEUR AND STRATEGIC PREPARATION

An unprepared field will make a frustrated Farmer.

Likewise, lack of good and affective preparation will always leads to business failure.

Effective preparation is the guarantee for your desired business success. What you don't prepare for, you cannot successfully partake of.

Business pursuit without effective preparation is a journey to frustration. Time spent in preparation is therefore time invested not wasted.

Every great business ventures is preceded by a dutiful preparation. The more detailed your preparation, the more distinguished your result.

Zig Ziglar says, "Success occurs when opportunity meets preparation." He also adds that a spectacular preparation precedes spectacular performance.

Preparation will refine your talent as gold. It will increase your ability to succeed and be productive in all that you do.

As a business woman, for you to succeed greatly in business, you must keep developing and maximizing your talent through effective preparation. Even if your current level has brought you a measure of success in business, you must not rest on your oars. It is not your gift that makes you a success; it is preparing yourself for opportunities to use them.

Marilyn Munroe attributes the major reason for her business success to preparation, or be ready. "Before everything else, getting ready, is the secret of success."

Calvin Klein, top fashion designer once said, "Possibilities always exist. It's always out there if you really want it and have the talent and are prepared for the hard work and challenges. Then any new designer can achieve something greater that I have achieved or Ralph Lauren or anyone else.

MAXIMUM EFFECTIVENESS.

To ensure maximum effectiveness and the fullest realization of your vision, you must commit yourself to necessary preparation. Because preparation attracts opportunity. You cannot be over-prepared; you are more likely to be severely under prepared. And inadequate preparation produces inadequate results.

Many businesses are largely victims of lack preparation.

Thomas Edison said, "Good fortune is what happens when opportunity meets with preparation.

Every business is at the mercy of preparation.

Because you can't get frustrated with facts. If you are trying to get ready when you are supposed to be ready, you are late.

An entrepreneur must be well prepared.

FACT FINDING MISSION

Strategic preparation is appropriate arrangement of facts. If you don't do mental work, you will end up doing menial work. In fact- finding mission, you identify what you have, and what you don't have. You examine the manpower, the money and the time at hand and you go ahead to make wise use of all you have at hand.

If you prepare very well for success in business and take practical steps towards implementation, there is no way you will not succeed?

5

WOMEN, PASSION AND BUSINESS SUCCESS.

Always bear in mind that your own resolution to succeed is more important than any other one thing –Abraham Lincoln.

As a female entrepreneur you must have a determination and passion to excel in business. You must be known for being a woman of determination.

Passion is what drives you forward in business. Passion is what makes you go to bed late and wake up very early. For you to build a successful business, You must be passionate about building a business. Passion will help you endure the challenges of the entrepreneurial process. Without passion forget about building a business.

Entrepreneurial success is for the hungry. Women who want to be an achiever by all means.

Passion is to crave or long for something with intensity. Passion is an essential requirement for business success. It is a burning desire to be special and do something extraordinary with your life.

The starting point of all accomplishments is passion. Keep this in mind. Feeble desire brings feeble results; Just as a small amount of fire makes a small amount of heat.

Be passionate about your business. Act from your passions. To experience great success you must want your business dream to be fulfilled because you will only be remembered in life for your passion .you must move towards the achievement of your vision with determination. Let it become an obsession. Put everything you've got inside that dream. That's where results will begin to come.

TURNING YOUR PASSION INTO MEGA BUSINESS.

Nothing can never stop a woman with a passion. One of the women that carry the greatest influence among the youth of Nigeria nations and world at large is pastor (Mrs.) Bimbo Odukoya of blessed memory. Mrs. Bimbo Odukoya has done tremendously so well in ministry not because of she knew so much but because she is passionate about what she knows. She has got the passion that flows from her sense of purpose to convey her message.

Mrs. Bimbo Odukoya possesses a great passion to bless the people of her generation. She has got passion to see the lives of her listener's blossom. They tried to stop Nelson Mandela but because of his passion he won. He was imprisoned for 27years in the process of trying to secure independence for his nation and freedom from colonial oppression. He eventually won the independence for his country and returned from person to become the first black president of the nation of South Africa. The secret to the outstanding success of Dr Mandela was that he was passionate and ready to pay the price to accomplish his goal.

Passion means you'll move forward even in the face of opposition. Passion means in disappointment you will still move forward.

Passion means that you have found something not only to live for but to die for. If you are going after your dream for your life, the question is how hungry are you?

To be successful in business you need to have a passion' not casual interest. Lack of passion make's people give up easily. It was the passion of being a world recognized scientist that drove Albert Einstein and Isaac Newton and all those acknowledge scientists to persists and persevere in their researches and Theories until a breakthrough was found. It was the passion of being the greatest inventor in America that drove Thomas Edison to spend long months before he could perfect incandescent electric lamp and despite the fact that he failed more than 10,000 times, that passion carried him to the discovery for which he was searching.

TURN YOUR PASSION INTO PROFIT

Harvard most distinguished professor, William James wrote ''in almost any subject, your passion for the subject will save you.

If you care enough for a result you will certainly attain it. If you wish to be good, you will be good. If you wish to be rich you will be rich. If you wish to be successful, you will be successful. Only that you must really wish those things and wish them with exclusiveness and not wish one hundred other incompatible thing just as strongly. What you are not willing to pursue you don't respect. And what you don't respect, you will never attract. Therefore you need to turn your passion loose by doing something about it something   practical and positive. Don't wait for a perfect condition because a perfect condition may never come. Start doing something about your life passion now.

6

WOMEN, PLANNING, GOAL SETTING AND BUSINESS SUCCESS.

Planning is the first step for moving your business objective from dream stage to reality. Planning is the key to business success. Your ideas, no matter how noble and great it is, will not see the light of the day without proper and strategic planning. If your dream or ideas has no plan or projection for effective execution, it is doomed for failure. As a matter of fact, someone one said; if you fail to plan, you have planned to fail.

Planning is the orderly and systematic arrangement of things by reasoning in order to achieve your objective. Using your brain as a female entrepreneur is one of the master keys to dignity and success in business. Planning is a major key and it always guarantees successful living.

Excellence business planning can be defined as the systematic arrangement of tasks in their proper order.

A WOMAN OF SUBSTANCE

Effective planning will help you to overcome many business challenges and win many battles in life and business.

Mary kay ash is one of the most successful women in America, worth more than $500 million. She is a super achiever. She said, every morning she invest time in creating a plan. She chooses six tasks she will accomplish each day. She works on task one as far as she can move it. Then she never works on tasks six until she has finished everything she can do on the first five.

Take time and do your home work, prepare in private. Do not just rush to take on a project or carry out a task without first carefully evaluating the cost.

Do not embark on business project without considering the best way to carry it out. If it is possible, sleep and meditate on your goal that appears to be extremely difficult to achieve. Resist the temptation to rush into action. Patience and wisdom are virtue to be respected and honored in business.

Action without planning is the cause of every failure. Therefore, go into your vision with your eyes open and good strategies along with it. Don't allow your vision to be watered down or end in failure. Well – defined and properly pursued vision will definitely make you a woman of success.

Planners accomplish great thing in business.

5. BASIC STEPS IN BUISNESS PLANNING

1. Setting objective

In business planning, you need to set or determine your objective. What do you want to achieve. You should outline the goals of the business and how these goals will be accomplished.

2. Organizing of strategies

You must put in place the arrangement that will help you to achieve your set objectives. You must put into consideration the how that will lead to best advantages result within limited time.

In the formulation of strategies, you must make sure you don't assume. You must avoid assumption. Strategies may be successful today but using the same strategies for the same task tomorrow may not succeed. As you write the plan, problems you might not have thought of before will be uncovered.

3. Procedures

This refers to the method of carrying out objective, strategies and assignments

4. Programmes.

This has to do with the steps involved in executing the objectives whether long or short term objectives.

You must develop a systematic arrangement that you will put in place that will help you to ultimately realize your business goal.

5. Budgeting.

In Business planning, budgeting can be defined as the statement of expected result that is mapped out both in momentary and hourly time. You must do this to eliminate waste of money and time.

10 QUESTIONS EVERY FEMALE ENTERPRENEUR MUST ASK ABOUT BUSINESS PLANNING.

What kind of business am I going into?

Let say what you want to do is to set up a restaurant. What kind of restaurant? Is it fast food Centre, intercontinental restaurants or local dishes canteen.

Is there a market?

Are there people in the neighborhood who love to eat the kind of food I want to offer or can be persuaded to love it. Because you cannot open a Chinese restaurant in a slum and expect people to patronize you in a large quantity.

Is there any competition?

Are there other restaurants in the neighborhood? How are they doing? How many are there? Do they have many customers waiting? Do they open for long hours? Are their customers satisfied?

What is my offering?

Why will people patronize my restaurant instead of using the others? What is the difference I wish to make? How do I plan to compete and to do better than the competitor? is it in the quality of service or food variety, or ambience of the restaurant or in pricing because the success or failure of your business will depend a lot on how successful you are at fixing the price.

What will it cost to set up my restaurant of my dream?

The cost of different items that I will need to set up the restaurant. Rent of the restaurant, cost of designing and decoration, cost of the equipment (one by one) e. t. c.

You must know the capital required and how it will be raised. Don't assume, be very sure.

Do I need caterers?

How many? What will they be paid? How will I recruit them? By advertisement? Head hunting? What should be their level of experience?

How do I plan to raise all the money?

From my savings, borrow from my family, friends or relation? Do I need to borrow from the banks or I will rather invite other people to invest in the business? So what is the size of equity and what is the size of debt? In the world of business, borrowing is inevitable because every business needs sufficient fund to survive.

Who are to patronize my restaurant?

How will they be reached? What price will they be prepared to pay? What quantity will they buy before you make a profit? How long will it take them to buy quantity?

Do you know the entire requirement for your line of business?

Make sure you settle all documentation and legalities.

What are the financial projections?

What kind of profit or loss will be made in the next

four to six years? How soon can I or my other investors recover their investment? What will the business look like in two of four years and what kind of assets or liability will the business have?

7

THE 21st CENTURY WOMAN ENTERPRENEUR

This is the jet age. Why? It is the information age. We live in a time where everything is moving at high speed. As a 21st century female entrepreneur, your mission is to have a global relevance. This generation has witnessed a great change in the area of science, technology, entertainment, communication, education and so on. The world has been reduced to a global village.

This is not the era of analog but a digitalize operation. We are in the era of information technology. These significant changes demand a new approach and method for effective business activities. Therefore it will take a well –informed, globally minded, well trained purpose driven entrepreneur to make a difference in our fast changing world.

5 QUALITIES OF 21st CENTURY FEMALE ENTERPRENEUR

EXPOSURE

The 21st century female entrepreneur must be an exposed woman. The more you expose yourself, the more you get the most out of life and business. The company you keep and the book you read will determine your business future. It is your level of exposure that largely determines your level of attainment. Positive exposure is a great asset in your quest for excellence in life and business.

Every outstanding female entrepreneur is known to be a committed reader. Exposure has no substitute in your quest for success. Expose yourself to knowledge; Expose yourself to Good books expose yourself to educational and inspirational CDS. The better your brain, the greater your gain.

EDUCATION.

Education is a process of acquiring information in a given area. Education is the greatest need of the hour. The reason why many businesses are grounded is because many people running such business are not properly educated on how to run a successful business. The kind of education I mean here is not just going to school, because what is the essence of feasibility studies without feasibility result; but it's about the one that is practical and applicable education.

Dr John Hibben, a university don in United States of America defined education as the ability to meet life's situation. Many women have started a business without having the right information on how to go about it. Without knowing what you must do to achieve success, you may die in your present spot.

EMPOWERMENT

When you are well exposed and educated, it will create a thirst to do and achieve great things in life and business – and that is why you need to be empowered.

No matter how intellectual you are, Negative spiritual forces won't let you go without demonstration of positive supernatural. your education or your money makes no difference. Power is the principal requirement to excel in this generation.

You must constantly be in fellowship with God to be empowered.

EXCELLENCE.

As a 21st century female entrepreneur, you must be a woman of Excellence. Excellence is constant improvement. It is doing small things well. We are in the era of quality service. Excellence will promote your business. Quality work is everything. Determine today to become absolutely excellence at what you do. Commit to doing your business the very best way possible. Set an excellent life style as your standard, continually strive to improve.

EXPLOITS.

Exploits means something of note. That is, something you can't stop thinking about. Something that make news. A 21st century female entrepreneur is a woman of exploit. You must impart and add value on the life of the people.

8

WOMEN AND ORGANISATION SKILL

Organization is a system or an orderly set of people with common goal and objectives. It is a group of individual, systematically united to do a certain work.

In this part of the world, a lot of people believe women cannot successful run an organization, especially business organization. They claimed women are emotional while men are logical. But as 21st century female entrepreneur, it is possible to run a world class business empire. All you need is to learn the basic principles that guides or build an effective business organization.

One of the major reasons why many businesses fail and collapse is because of lack effective organization .someone said if you don't organize, you will agonize. Many business owners thought in order to be successful in business, you need to have an idea, have some money in your account, and have a passion. But unless you have also a well thought organizational structure, a strong well discipline administrative team and a reliable body of co-workers, success in business can be a mirage.

Organization and system building are essential for your business success. They are stepping stone for you to be a success. Great success in business is knowing what only you can do and what needs to be delegated to others. As the business grows, it becomes too big for only one person to run even if you are a musician. When you don't learn to delegate and organize your personal life, people working together with you and your finances correctly, you will AGONIZE.

Many businesses have collapsed due to a lack of a well-planned financial policy. There is a need to break down your business objectives into small bits to avoid nervous and emotional breakdown. The ability of every business owner demands that you have a good organization and system in place.

Lack of good organization in any business venture brings confusion, which slows down progress of any endeavor. Good organization enhances good thinking and effective business.

PROCESS OF BUILDINGS AN EFFECTIVE BUSINESS ORGANIZATION

Establish a clear goal and objectives.

What do you want to achieve? As a business woman, you have to establish a clear mission. Give everybody working with you a clear sense of purpose and direction. **Establish a clear purpose.**

Business leaders are visionary; they chart the course for others to follow.

Design a structure around your mission.

You must learn to structure around your business purpose. Start small and expand the structure as growth comes. Also, develop structure for the next phase of your business.

Keep the structure simple and very flexible.

Learn to keep your structure very simple. Don't allow it to be complex. It must be very flexible; because structure is like clothes. As you grow the size of your clothes changes, like wise as your business grow, the structure also changes.

Always look for opportunities to expand your business facility to serve more customers.

Train the people who will run the system

Do training regularly in your organization. Because when people know better they will act better. If you cannot personally train them by yourself, hire experts to come and do the training for them.

Always design strategic training to improve skills.

Have a mentor who has successful and effectively built a system.

This is the major key to the achievement of many successful people. There is no new thing under heaven. Everything is a pattern of something else. There are women who have built mighty business empire, follow in their footsteps and you will get to where they have been.

9

ACQUIRE ALL RELEVANT INFORMATION.

The law of integrative complexity says that the individual who can integrate and use the greatest amount of information in any field soon rises to the top of that field –Brian Tracy.

We live in a world of information. A world where having the right information matters a great deal. In today's world of business, relevant information will make the different between your present state and your future. Great accomplishment in life and business answers to knowledge.

The baseline for super achievement in your business is knowledge. The more you know the more capacity for success you develop. Your ability for Great success in business is largely determined by the knowledge you are expose to. However not only the exposure, but the application of the knowledge is also crucial.

So, the extra ordinary mind you possess is your greatest asset in business. I should let you know at this junction that success in business world of today is not just having a great passion or profitable ideas but having a sound mind as well. This is because without updating, there will be outdating. If you don't want your business to be outdated, keep updating.

Woman, you don't celebrate beauty in business world, you are only exalted by knowledge. If your competitor happened to know better than you do, then you are retired from your leadership position. Because a leader is a woman doing great things. It is your mental capacity that determines the size of your result. The difference between a successful business woman and failure is in what they know and also in what they do with what they know.

MARY KAY'S SECRET.

A man by the name of Glenn bland was looking

around the bookshop in an airport one day and he saw a book about wealth creation. In the book, the author claim to have studied the lives of over 500 millionaires and that the same practical steps it takes for anyone to break out of poverty into unimaginable wealth was clearly outlined in that book. Bland held tight to the book, think and grow rich" by Napoleon Hill, bought and read it all through his Journey on the plane.

He went a step further to believe the book and vowed he was going to obey the clear, practical steps to wealth outlined in it. Bland also gave himself a goal of starting an insurance company and growing it to be the most successful in America within five years. He reached his goal and exceeded it. He became a multi-millionaire and a philanthropist sponsoring many positive organization and churches.

Another man by the name of A.L Williams got hold of the same book read and believed it, and went ahead to create a special market strategy. He started a business in life insurance, reached and exceeded his goal and his company had a turnover of $89 billion.

Mary Kay ash was a lady who got a copy of this same book, read it and started her own business, selling women's cosmetics. She is one of the famous business women's on earth. She is worth over $2 billion Dollars and her business is over $100 billion. Through the reading of the book, she was able to set up a marketing scheme for her products and today Mary Kay's voice is the most powerful female voice in business. She has over 700, 000 women selling Mary Kay's cosmetics all over the world.

HOW TO GENERATE PROFITABLE IDEAS

Every committed reader will never lack ideas to succeed in business and a wining idea is the starting point of all riches. Books are collection of facts, information, ideas and figures. When a woman commits herself to acquiring relevant information in the area of her passion, she will be opened to a world of ideas which will ultimately lead to creation of timely products and services. Then success will embrace her.

 Ignorance incapacitates. It can limit your quest for success in business. If you don't learn anything new today. Tomorrow will be no different. Be willing to go for every bit of information that can enhance and maximize your business and you will be launched into greater things in business.

3 SIMPLE WAYS OF ACQUIRING INFORMATION

BY READING.

Every business mogul is a celebrated reader. A woman who does not read does not have an advantage over a woman who cannot read. Many successful women in our world today are committed readers. The secret of successful people is in their stories.

The secret of how some celebrated business people overcame the various challenges and obstacles that confronted them in the past can be found in books, magazines and business Journals.

You have countless information represented by Biographies and auto biographies of successful business people. Many years of experience can be transmitted through one book. Books contain solution to difficulties.

Books offer you a great opportunity to relate with

successful business people.

There are many great business women who have achieved more than you in business. You can improve the quality of your life and business by relating with such people through their books.

Listen to educative and informative audio programs.

As you listen to audio programme, you learn the message. You acquire the information. You tap into the knowledge content and you also receive great insights. Many people have become millionaires through the miracle of listening to CDS.You can become one of the most successful business women Just by listen to educative and informative audio CDS by experts.

Attending seminars and business workshop.

The third key of acquiring knowledge is to attend every course and seminar you can possibly find that can help you to be a better entrepreneur. Participate in educative

10

WOMEN AND BUSINESS APPRENTICESHIP

Every business achievement demands a high level training.

Career success is a product of excellent training and commitment. It is for this reason that I strongly advocate sound business training for everyone that wants to go into entrepreneurship.

Every woman who cares to make a great Impact in business must necessarily pass through this exercise.

Business Apprenticeship can be defined as an opportunity for obtaining adequate training in a specific career or profession. Its essence is to acquire exposure or knowledge in that particular field. Knowledge is a medium of communicating information, while apprenticeship is a way of imparting skills and technical know-how. Apprenticeship offers practical and applicable education.

Personal knowledge cannot take the place of Apprenticeship. Successful entrepreneurial skill is acquired through training.

As a career woman, you may have some business qualities and traits but if not subject to adequate training, the best of it cannot be realized. Experts in any career are made via training for skills and expertise. The ''self –made '' attitude has destroyed so many aspiring business women.

BE QUALITY DRIVEN

'Every Job is a self-portrait of the person who did it. Many times the difference in failure and success is doing something nearly right or doing it exactly right. Autograph your work and business with Quality". – unknown

I believe strongly that people should not venture into new business until they have patiently gone through a period of Apprenticeship no matter how short. We have had enough of business failures. You cannot afford to add more, more than 80 percent of new business closes down or disappear within the first two years of startup according to Brian Tracy, and many large, established companies go bankrupt or are taken over by other organization every year. The reason is this many are doing what they are not trained for.

It was not until Esther in the Bible underwent apprenticeship under mordecai, her uncle, that she could be trusted with the responsibility of being promoted. As a career woman, Quality should become your watch word. Quality spells out the lasting effect on any business.

We are in an impatient age where an average Individual wants instant result. You must realize that every instant result you see in other successful women today has gone through a hidden and slow process of making. Sometimes you may succeed in getting instant results but what about its lasting effect and sustenance? Any woman that is too much in a hurry not to go through apprenticeship doesn't have a guaranteed future in business.

GENDER IS IRRELEVANT

Business success is in not in age, colour or gender. It is in the expertise gathered as a result of the training you subject yourself to. Achievement is in what you know and what you are able to do with your hands. You cannot do anything with your hands successful unless you learn it. How do you learn? Join in the apprenticeship programme.

HAVING A DEGREE IS NOT A SUBTITUTE.

Excellence in one field of business is not transferable to another. Having a first class degree in micro –biology does not make you an automatic success in music. Because you have a master degree in business administration does not guarantee you success in entertainment industry. Every trade has its peculiarities. Every field no matter how insignificant it may appear requires a unique and particular attention and training to get the best out of it. This is to simply say that you cannot transfer your skill in any field to another. Your training in a particular field does not qualify you for mastery in another field.

PRINCIPAL SOURCE OF EXPERINCE.

Experience is the breast milk of a successful vision.

The benefit of involving others in your vision is your instant accessibility to experience, progress, knowledge and wisdom.

Experience doesn't equal knowledge. The latter is higher and usually more current than the former. This is not to say, however, that you can substitute knowledge for experience. Experience serves as a control valve for the application of knowledge.

Knowledge drives you into putting in the best you can, but experience teaches you how not to immediately accept an unfavorable response as final. Perseverance and stamina are product of experience.

An untrained person, after using a tool(acquired via knowledge)and it doesn't work, may easily be discouraged, not knowing that there could be other methods of accomplishing the task.

This is not so for a woman who has picked her lessons on apprenticeship. She has learnt from her trainer how to turn to another tool in case the previous one fail. Experience teaches you to stay around your business until you find a way forwards instead of turning your back at it in failure and despair. Knowledge is power, but experience is an irresistible force when applied with wisdom.

Business Apprenticeship is the principal source of Experience.

11

HOW TO GROW YOUR BUSINESS AS A WOMAN

Stagnation is failure. Someone who remains on one spot is actually going backwards without knowing. Failure is quick to catch up with such person and overtake those who are not making steady progress in business.

It is not a crime to start small but it is a crime, punishable by slow death to remain small. No matter the level of success you have experienced in the time past, if you are not advancing and progressing. You are dying.

Bill gates turned around the face of the computer industry via the principle of business progress and improvement. The initial versions of the graphic based operating system, "windows" which his company developed were commercial failure and also full of bugs. However, Bill gates continued to develop himself and micro soft continued to improve by correcting the bugs until window 3;1 version, which achieved considerable success. The next version was released after window 95,which recorded tremendous commercial success because it was a great improvement over the previous version.

BUSINESS PROGESS AND IMPROVEMENT is your guarantee for continuous and unlimited business success.

Woman, I want to encourage you to avoid the syndrome of '' success. Destination disease" that is, the "I have arrived attitude." As long as you are green you are growing but as soon as you arrive you will start to rot.

For you to survive, thrive and succeed in a fast changing world, you will have to get back to the drawing board to find new ways to do what you are doing faster and better and also to carry out research to make your system of operation more efficient. You will have to study and learn aggressively on how to enlarge your marketing potentials by penetrating new markets and how to increase your income base. After five years of operation the ford company, Henry ford was producing six thousand, one hundred and eighty – one cars in a year. But he was not satisfied with this result. A few years after so many research and discovery, the company adopted a revolutionary assembly line method and soon produced thirty five thousand model t ford cars a year. Not too long after that, Ford was building four thousand cars a day.

Take practical steps on how to grow big and make progress. Making progress in business involve 4 major steps.

4 MAJOR STEPS TO BUSINESS PROGRESS

Forgetting those things that are behind.

Many people are unduly attached to the past. When you refuse to move beyond yesterday, you cannot advance into great future that lies ahead of you. To make business progress you must let go of what is behind. Not just past failures but your −past successes too. Do not dwell on your past achievement, move on. Do not allow yesterday's failure to limit you either. Each day brings along its fresh opportunities to try again. When you are locked up in the past, you are in capacitated. But when you choose to put the past behind you, you are released to explore new frontiers. You are ready to access greater things.

Reaching forth.

That is dealing with your present challenges. There is no challenge on your path that is superior to your mind power. No challenge is bigger than you. Nothing is too strong to defeat you.

Focus on the future.

Your future is your picture. The happiest people are those who live in their future. No matter where you are now, no matter where you have been before, there is always a higher level of opportunities. There is always a higher quality of life.

Learn to press (pursuit)

You cannot enjoy business progress until you press to it. Everything precious thing comes out of pressure. If you dodge the pressure, you miss the precious because pressing is the prize for every business progress. Always shun short- cuts. There is no short cut to business breakthrough.

12

SIMLPE WAYS TO RAISE CAPITAL FOR YOUR BUSINESS

Money is the greatest attribute of riches, the stuff that makes the rest possible.- Robert brown.

As a female entrepreneur, you must approach business with abundant mentality and never let go that mentality. When it comes to raising capital for your business, your belief system is very important. If you think in your mind there is no money then you wouldn't be able to raise necessary capital for your business, but if you have the mentality of abundance, then doors of opportunities will be opened for you to be able to generate capital to run your business.

In raising capital for your business, the first thing you must have to be successful at is the wealth mindset. When you have the right mind set, it will allow you to be able to see money and opportunities everywhere.

We live in an abundant universe where there is enough supply of money for all those who really want it. Avoid every limiting belief that may hinder you to take proper action in actualizing your business dream. Destroy every ''mental stronghold, '' a thought that tells you that there is no money to finance your business or to achieve your desire result.

If you really desire to raise capital to run your business and you do not have limiting beliefs, you will always find a way to get it.

This is very important! You cannot afford to have scarcity mindset and enjoy financial breakthrough in business. Always have the mindset that opportunity to raise capital is available. Not only available, but also obtainable.

HOW TO RAISE CAPITAL

Have a solid business plan.

The no 1 way to raise capital is to have a solid business plan. Write a business prospectus. Your business prospectus must contain your resume or your experience. write a detail of how the money will be used. It must contain project cost and your marketing research. How much to spend for take – off. In writing a good business plan, state the benefits to your investor. It may be percentage of profit or part of ownership of the business. You must have a solid business plan to be able to attract investor into your business.

Personal savings.

Personal saving should be what a serious prospective entrepreneur must do when venturing into business. To show you believe in your business dream and ideas, you have to put your own money first as your personal contribution.

Your personal assets.

There is nothing bad in selling some of your valuable asset that you are not really using now to be able to raise capital for your dream business. The ability to turn personal assets like landed property, stock, jewelries, car and so on to cash will take the stress out of the capital raising endeavour.

Sometimes, you may need to sell that expensive handset, gold chain e. t. c. to just be able to fund your business. Someone is always ready to pick them up at a very affordable and reasonable price to get you started.

4. Your friends and your relations.

As a married woman, your husband can be very helpful in raising capital. Good family member always find it difficult to watch their relatives stranded in life and business endeavor due to lack of capital. The next time you need capital to run your business, Ask your spouse, friends, and relations. But you must have a good track record.

5. Money broker.

These are people who know people who have money and they are ready to connect you, but they will take a commission.

6. Mentor funding

Mentors are like parents. They love to assist their children to achieve result. If you have a mentor you are relating with, don't be proud to approach him or her for assistance. A genuine mentor will always be happy to support you with his or her resources

7. You can advertise and ask for help.

A popular movie star recently advertises on face book that he needed an investor to invest in his new movie. And within few days, A lady contacted him that she will like to invest #10,000 ($90,000) in his new film.

You too, can advertise that you need investors.

8. Thrift savings / co – operatives:

This is common among market women.

One of the major reasons for thrift and co – operative saving is to find or expand business .

Thrift saving / co – operative is best among those that know themselves, and most time are in the same type of business, tribe or environment.

9. Gratuity and pension

Most time, elderly people that started their own business start with their pension or gratuity. Gratuity is money that is given to employees when they leave their job while pension is an amount of money paid regularly by a government or company to someone who is considered to be too old or too ill to work. The amount payable in most cases goes up according to the number of years spent in the organization.

10. Partnership funding.

This is what is called strategic alliance or a master mind funding. You can partner with anyone that has the money and the interest to fund your business. The trouble with this is that most people with business idea often fail to realize that money is as critical as the idea itself. In other words, while the business idea is good and could make tons of money, the money the other party will also contribute to take the idea to the market place is at this point also very important. If the business owner fails to recognize this fact and keeps insisting that she would have more shares in the business than the person providing the cash, then there will be no partnership.

11. Internet Sources

This is a powerful means for generating capital for your business idea if you know how to access it. There is immediate capital you can access on the internet. When you log in, you are provided an exhaustive list of various types of people. The categories range from the size of the money needed, for what project the money is needed and for what time frame.

The internet will give you the way to access the sources and everything you need to know about them.

12. DEBT FINANCING

You can also borrow the money and promise to pay it back over a set period of time at a set rate of interest. There is hardly a successful business mogul who didn't at a point borrow some money to improve and advance her business. You can negotiate with good banks who can give you good loan to run your business; a lot of people keep their money in the banks without knowing what to do with it. You just approach the bank manager and tell him/her about your proposed investment and once they see seriousness in you, they will assist you

"Behind each millionaire hides a frenzied borrower Aristotle onasis

13. Angel Financing

Angels are private investors (non professional financing sources) who are interested in investing in new businesses for a variety of reasons, from friendship to a desire to support entrepreneurship in a given field.

14. NON-GOVERNMENT ORGANIZATION (NGO)

These are institution set up as non – commercial unit, nonprofit making to advance identified objectives. Some of these organizations provide assistance for business start up and similar Endeavour.

Several NGO's abound to take care of interest of those who need finance in virtually all areas of business

13

HOW TO SUCCEED IN THE MARKET PLACE

Nothing happens until a sale takes place. Red motley

Marketing is the art of reaching out to the market (customer) with your ideas, products and service to gain patronage. This is probably one of the most neglected aspects of entrepreneurial success.

As a female entrepreneur, your ability to identify and reach out to your target audience with your product or service is critical to your success in business. Because products and service are sold, not bought.

If your idea, product or service is good but don't have a solid marketing strategy, failure is almost inevitable. Conversely, if you have a second – rate product or services with a well implemented excellent marketing strategy, success is certain

Strategy and effective marketing is the key to great business success. Because it is the engines that drives your business.

"It is an economic fact that in a competitive market place, the effective of marketing is the primary determinant of business success."- Sonia rappaport

DEFINE YOUR MARKET

A market is the external collection of customers and buyers which is the ultimate sources of business and without which, there is no business

In a country as populated as Nigeria, with over 160 million inhabitants; it is important to adequately define your market and identify them in order to properly reach them your with product and services.

In defining your market, there are 3 basics question you must ask yourself.

Who they are.

This has to do with defining the populace based on age, gender, marital status, occupation, family size and nationality.

What they are like

This has to do with the classification of people according to their attitude, belief, interest and opinions.

Where they live.

This has to do with classifying people based on where they live and location.

GO TO WHERE FISHES ARE

Many business and organization are struggling for many years just because they are located in the wrong place. You need to go where fishes are. There is no point fishing for sharks in the pond, go to where your fishes are.

Take your products or services to where your

market is i.e. where you can locate people who are likely to use your products and services.

Never keep your products or services at a place while waiting for potential customers to come. The women who have made the most impact in the market place today are the ones, who always venture into thickest regions of the market. Whereas their counter parts who always prefer to remain in calm environment hardly never catch something in abundance.

THE POWER OF PERSUATION

Persuasion is the ability to influence others it is the ability of getting others to support your recommendation. For you to succeed greatly in the market place, you must be able to influence customers decision and also to convince customer that they will be better off with your product than they would be with the money necessary to buy the product. The power of persuasion is an important strategy for market success.

FOCUS ON BENEFITS.

Benefits are solution to the people's day to day

problem. By simply improving, enhancing

and emphasizing your product or service benefits, You can double your sales, increase customer loyalty and sustain the attention of your customers.

Customers are always excited when they can perceive that your product offer them a benefit. Therefore, always seek to define, communicate and emphasize the benefits of your product and services to your potential customers.

SETTING THE RIGHT PRICE

Never allow your workers to indulge in profiteering but always to efficiently present your product or services. Pricing to a new product or someone that is just starting business can be a million dollar idea. Find out the level of pricing in your industry before placing any price on your product or service. Let your pricing be such that large number of your potential customers can afford.

OTHER BOOKS BY ISAAC GIWA.

1. Million dollar generating habit
2. Digging your diamond mine
3. Your mind is a miracle
4. Be a super achiever
5. Provoking your harvest
6. Seizing the moment
7. Secrets of financial success
8. Changing your world
9. Get ready...money cometh
10. Secrets for business success
11. Simple ideas on how to create your own miracle
12. Changing impossible situation
13. The secrets of highly successful people
14. 5 great ways to succeed in your own business
15. How to receive instance answer to your prayer
16. Becoming a proof producer
17. Be a success superstar
18. How to guarantee your success 100%
19. War against marital delay
20. War against wickedness
21. 12 rules for total life prosperity
22. Success handbook for single ladies
23. The business success principle
24. Success handbook for single men
25. The healing book
26. Success handbook for every woman

55. Overcoming sexual bondage
56. Praying for your husband
57. Family deliverance prayer
58. Success handbook for everyman
59. Achieving career success
60. Success strategies for teens
61. Achievement secrets 101
62. How to achieve financial freedom
63. How to build a successful relationship
64. Failure is not final
65. Simple ways to get answers to your prayer
66. Start with nothing & achieve great success
67. Successful businessmen handbook
68. How to make your business work
69. Business success strategy that works
70. Business breakthrough ideas
71. Achieving outstanding business success
72. How to start & build your own business
73. Financial freedom for every woman
74. Wisdom
75. What every singles needs to know
76. The business woman's handbook
77. Wisdom for single ladies
78. How to be a successful female entrepreneur
79. Great rules for women in the work place
80. Career success for today's woman
81. How to start & profit with your own idea
82. A successful woman handbook
83. Woman power

GET CONNECTED

God is our power source.

He is the well-spring of wisdom. Once He comes into your heart a profound relationship with wisdom and power becomes inevitable. He is the foundation of grace. Without the flow of his divine grace, we malfunction and life becomes tedious. His graceful support is still available for you today.

He wants to help you in achieving your dreams and desires in life. He has helped many others. He can help you. So, my friends you too can enjoy his remarkable support today!

All you need to do is to accept Him as your Lord and Saviour. You will experience a change in your heart.

Say this prayer with me right now:

"Lord Jesus, thank you for dying for me on the cross". I turn to you to establish a relationship with you today. I ask that you forgive me my sins and cleanse me with your previous blood.

Let your life, grace and wisdom begin to find fulfillment. In my life today. Rule in my heart today as my Lord and personal Saviour.

Thank you for saving me.

OUR MISSION

To let you know that God wants you to prosper and succeed.

To help you discover the tremendous potential the creator has graciously invested in your life.

To impact into your life the manifold wisdom of God.

To ensure your total deliverance from failure and poverty.

To release through effective prayer, the power of God to effect positive change in your circumstances.

YOUR LETTER IS VERY IMPORTANT TO ME

You are a special person to me and I believe that you are special to God.

I want to help you in any way possible. Do you have any prayer request? Write me when you need an intercessor to pray for you.

Let be hear from you when you are facing spiritual needs or experiencing a conflict in your business, marriage and career.

When you write, my staff and I will pray over your letter. I will write you back to help you receive the miracle you need.

I will look forward to your letter.

For more information, please contact;

ISAAC GIWA

Wisdom Impartation Ministries Int'l

P.O. box 621, Ikeja, Lagos-Nigeria.

Phone: 234-802-314-7715, 234-803-666-5662

E-Mail: wisdomimpart@yahoo.com

isaacgiwabooks@gmail..com

WILL YOU BECOME A PARTNER WITH MY MINISTRY?

Your Financial Seeds Are So Powerful In Helping Heal Broken Lives. When You Sow Into the Work of God, Miracle Harvest Are Guaranteed

*Supernatural protection. (Malachi 3:10)

*Supernatural favour (Luke 6:38)

*Supernatural Health (Isaiah (58:8)

*Supernatural wisdom & financial ideas. (Deuteronomy 8:18)

Sow your seed today, then focus your expectation for the -100 fold return! An unusual seed will always create an unusual harvest.

To Sow Your Seed Today

Pay Into Any:

Bank: Guarantee Trust Bank

Account Name: Isaac Giwa

Account Number: 0006808883

Or Call,

+234-8023147715

ISAAC GIWA

+234-8036665662

+234-8189800366

E-Mail: wisdomimpart@yahoo.com

P.O. Box 621, Ikeja, Lagos, Nigeria.

BOOK ENCOUNTERS

A lot of people have received their breakthroughs just by reading Dr. Isaac Giwa's books. His books are life-changing manual and anointed spiritual weapons with which many fought battles over Failure, Stagnation, Poverty, Hardship, Afflictions e.t.c., and won!

Read these:

The book "Money Cometh" has done wonders to my finances. I recommend it for anyone that wants to succeed in this peculiar environment of Africa. It's a must read.

Olayinka Aina, Author:

Enjoy A Superb Service Year"

Lagos-Nigeria

Your book is an inspiring one and very intellectual. It has taught me how to be wise financially.

Josephine Asare, Author:

"All About Your Dreams

Accra-Ghana

I have read your book titled "secret of BUSINESS

SUCCESS" I found the book quite educative, informative and above all it's a book that anybody that wants to succeed in business need to go through.

-Hassan Yusuf

Kaduna-Nigeria

Sir, the hunger and the burning to change my world have been eaten me up lately. Thank God for coming across your book "CHANGING YOUR WORLD" it's a booster.

Thanks.

-Michael A.

Lagos-Nigeria.